The
Developmental
<u>Dilemma</u>

Helping Parents Reclaim the Joy and Power of Youth Sport

Jay Harrison, PhD

Framing the Developmental Dilemma

Sport is a powerful resource in a child's development. It is one of the few places that offer opportunities for physical, cognitive, emotional, and social growth all in one. Sport helps children develop physical fitness, coordination, and motor skills. It also enhances cognitive functions such as problem-solving, strategic thinking, and concentration. Emotionally, sport has the capacity to boost self-esteem, resilience, and stress management. Socially, it fosters teamwork, communication, and leadership skills.

Yet today's youth sport landscape presents significant challenges for both children and parents. The expectations placed on young athletes to perform at exceptionally high levels have created a high-pressure environment that can be overwhelming. This pressure is leading children to become physically and emotionally exhausted from the relentless demands of training and competition at young ages. Self-esteem issues can also manifest, with young athletes often tying their self-worth to their performance. Toxic competition, driven by myopic parents and coaches focused solely on winning, further complicates the youth sport experience.

For parents, the stakes are high. They are often required to dedicate extensive time, money, and resources to support their children's athletic pursuits. The high stakes nature of youth sport leads parents to feel an overwhelming responsibility to provide every possible opportunity for their child's sporting success. This pressure can cause significant familial strain, even leading parents to inadvertently contribute to a toxic atmosphere without even knowing it. The pursuit of sporting success can drive parents to make decisions that may not always align with their child's best interests and overshadow the benefits that sport provides.

The developmental dilemma arises when parents must decide whether to prioritize an elite high-performance youth sport trajectory for their child or provide diverse experiences that foster a child's overall development. In today's youth sport environment, the developmental dilemma is a challenge faced by parents earlier and earlier in their child's sporting experience. Is your child going to try out for the travel team? Are they getting lessons? Are they going to camps to improve their skills? Do they have access to the best travel teams and schedules? Are they playing for the right coaches? Are they going to the right school? These are just some questions parents navigate as their children begin to explore and develop a budding interest and proficiency in a sport.

Wanting to provide their children every opportunity, parents often feel compelled to heavily invest in their child's sporting development, and if not, they may think they will stifle their child's athletic potential. This belief creates significant anxiety and fear in parents. They might feel as though their child's future success rests on their shoulders and with the opportunities they, as parents, can create. Parents may believe that if they don't provide every single opportunity and resource, that could be the difference between greatness and failure for their child.

Make no mistake: the world of competitive elite youth sport is very attractive. The outcomes of playing at a high level can be positive and desirable for both children and parents. These outcomes can include skill mastery at a young age, positive social and developmental attention from parents, peers, school teams, and the community, and the prestige that comes with early success. It presents an opportunity to be part of a competitive, exclusive, and successful environment.

As attractive as the competitive route may seem, some parents are uncomfortable with the demands it presents. It can be all-consuming, with intense training schedules, frequent competitions, financial burdens, and high-pressure situations. This lifestyle often requires families to commit countless hours to practice and competition and prioritize sport above other developmental opportunities and family priorities. Parents may aim to provide a more diverse childhood experience that includes a variety of experiences in the pursuit of a well-rounded development. So, what are parents to do?

The purpose of writing this book was to acknowledge the challenges of being a sports parent and, in doing so, empower parents to take control of their child's sports journey. It is to ensure that the decision to prioritize high-performance outcomes in youth sport or provide diverse experiences are informed decisions that truly serve their child's growth and enjoyment.

There is no "right" path. Whether early specialization or a more developmentally balanced approach—both have their merits and challenges. The key outcome of this book is to ensure that regardless of the path parents choose, there is alignment between the family's values, the child's interests and capabilities, and their broader developmental experience. The book offers a roadmap for parents that provides insights and perspective, along with practical strategies and a framework to ensure a child's sports experience is serving them in the best possible way.

Youth sport holds immense potential for positive experiences and personal growth. By adopting a proactive and informed approach, parents can transform sport into a powerful catalyst for their child's development, ensuring it nurtures growth and prepares them for a successful future.

The Specialization & Professionalization of Youth Sport

The developmental dilemma arises when parents must decide whether to focus on one competitive sport or provide a diverse childhood experience that includes different sports and recreational activities. This dilemma is fueled by several factors and belief systems that lead parents to invest heavily in their children's athletic endeavors early on, fearing that their child might miss out on the opportunity of becoming an elite athlete.

Early sport specialization refers to a trend where children focus on one sport at a very young age, often before the age of ten. It involves spending a significant amount of time and energy on the chosen sport at the expense of other activities, both in and out of sport. It is a relatively new phenomenon. For most of the past century, sports were unstructured, neighborhood-based activities for children. The focus was on fun, participation and enjoyment, not competition and performance. The mid-20th century saw a shift towards more organized youth sports, with forming local leagues and clubs. However, even then, the focus of these organizations was to provide children with opportunities for socialization, physical activity, and character development. Winning was a goal, but not the primary aim. While those who were athletically gifted still thrived, each sport only provided a limited opportunity for skill specific development—sport participation was seasonal.

The 1990s and early 2000s brought the professionalization of youth sports. Driven by changing societal norms, availability of resources (indoor golf dome, anyone?) and a competitive ethos, youth sport became big business. Today, youth sport is far removed from the neighborhood games of the past. With an emphasis on performance and winning, it has become a high-pressure endeavor for many children and parents, leading many to seek early specialization and year-round training.

With rigorous training schedules, intensive coaching, and high-stakes tournaments—youth sports have become increasingly structured and mirror elite and professional levels. Organized youth sport is now a multi-billion-dollar industry. Just to get an idea of the scope— in 2021 the youth and amateur sports industry had a direct spending impact of nearly $40 billion, with an expected growth rate of 9% year-over-year. According to a TD Ameritrade survey, 27% of parents spend more than $500 per month on their child's sporting activities. From private coaching and specialized training to equipment and apparel, to hotels and travel. The business of youth sports is vast and continues to grow—driven by providing younger players a more professionalized experience.

A predominant belief in sport parenting circles is that early specialization is the key to success. This idea is rooted in the notion that focusing on a single sport from a young age will enhance a child's ability to reach elite levels. Proponents of this approach argue that early specialization is needed to acquire the fundamental skills and techniques needed to excel at higher levels. This belief is often reinforced by success stories of athletes who have achieved greatness through intensive, single-sport training, creating a compelling narrative for parents. Many will use these athletes as role models to show that early specialization leads to long-term success. This message encourages parents and young athletes to believe that early specialization is the only way to reach their full athletic potential.

The trend of children specializing younger and younger has had profound effects on the developmental landscape.

With early specialization and access to resources, children's developmental trajectories are steep—they are getting really good, really fast—increasing the competition for developmental resources. To access the highest quality developmental resources now requires children to demonstrate advanced skill development at a young age. Thus, parents are driven to commit to a specialized sport development plan lest their child be left behind—the developmental dilemma in action.

And while early specialization produces more skilled athletes faster, one must ask: is it good for children?

With Specialization Comes Risks

It is common for many to promote early sport specialization as essential for cultivating elite athletes. To the naked eye, the results speak for themselves. Children with early exposure and enriched development environments in sport demonstrate a competitive advantage by acquiring advanced skills and techniques at a young age. These children gain more experience and practice in their sport, improving their performance rapidly.

However, researchers have documented that early sport specialization can have unintended negative consequences. Athletes who specialize early are more likely to experience a range of physical, emotional, and psychological problems. Overuse injuries are particularly common among young athletes who specialize in one sport due to the repetitive and intense nature of their training routines. This can lead to chronic pain, inflammation, and stress fractures, and a shortened athletic career.

Additionally, burnout is a significant risk. The intense training schedules and constant pressure to perform can lead to physical and emotional exhaustion. This exhaustion can cause a loss of passion for the sport, decreased motivation, and even dropout. The high demands placed on these young athletes can make them feel overwhelmed, leading them to disengage from the sport they once loved.

Early sport specialization has also been linked to negative psychological effects on young athletes. The pressure to succeed and meet high expectations can lead to anxiety, depression, and low self-esteem. Young athletes may feel an overwhelming sense of failure if they do not meet the high standards set by themselves, their coaches, or their parents. This pressure can cause severe stress, leading to mental health issues that can persist into adulthood.

Furthermore, the social environment within specialized sports can sometimes be toxic. The intense competition can lead to bullying, exclusion, and a lack of camaraderie among teammates. Young athletes might face social isolation if they are perceived as not performing up to par, which can further exacerbate feelings of anxiety and depression.

Specialization: Does it work?

As the youth sport industry continues to thrive, it's hard not to wonder: is early specialization in sport effective?

With the industry worth a whopping $19 billion, there must be concrete evidence to support the idea that starting young and specializing early leads to not only quicker development but also long-term athletic success. Is early specialization the path to athletic achievement or just a myth? The research is clear:

Early specialization does not increase a child's chances of reaching elite levels in sport.

Many studies have examined the developmental trajectories of elite athletes and have found that a more diverse range of sporting experiences in childhood are a greater predictor of long-term success in sport. One study, published in the British Journal of Sports Medicine, followed the developmental pathways of 835 male and female athletes across 10 sports over 10 years. The study concluded that athletes specializing in a sport before the age of 12 were less likely to achieve elite status compared to those who specialized later or participated in multiple sports. European researchers also analyzed the careers of 304 elite male footballers and found that players who specialized in soccer later (around 16) were more likely to become professionals than those who specialized at a younger age (before 12). In one of the largest studies completed on early sport specialization that surveyed over 3000 athletes found that the higher the level of achievement in sport (high school vs. collegiate vs. professional), the later the time of sport specialization.

What does it all mean?

While this is far from an exhaustive review of the literature, the message is clear: early sport specialization may help a child reach their top potential faster, but it does not necessarily help them go farther in their athletic career or lead to long-term success. Athletic talent—and sport development trajectory—cannot be predicted (very well, at least!) based on pre-pubescent development or performance. Rather, athletes who do have the talent and capacity to develop into elite athletes tend to benefit from more diverse sporting experiences in their youth. Playing multiple sports and having a diverse athletic background leads to better physical development, socialization, and mental well-being—and is associated with long-term athletic success. Though early specialization can enhance skill development, it is not a prerequisite to reach elite status in sport.

Let's All Just Take A Breath

The narrative that early sport specialization is the definitive path to elite athletic success has driven many parents to invest heavily in their children's sporting endeavors from a young age. However, research shows that early specialization does not necessarily increase a child's chances of reaching elite levels in sports. In reality, it is more likely to cause negative outcomes such as overuse injuries, burnout, and psychological stress. This realization should not dishearten parents but rather empower them to embrace a broader perspective on their child's sports journey.

The goal is not to dismiss early specialization outright but to ensure that any approach to youth sport—whether specialized or diversified— aligns with what is best for the child and that youth sport decisions are made with awareness of the benefits and consequences. Whether a child specializes early or enjoys a variety of activities, what matters most is that they feel supported, motivated, and happy. Let's all take a breath and remember that the journey through youth sports should be a joyful and fulfilling part of a child's development, not a source of undue stress or pressure. By doing so, parents can help their children cultivate a lifelong passion for sport, regardless of level of participation or success.

Let's talk about Parents

The conversation would not be complete without discussing the factors that motivate parents and how those factors contribute to the developmental dilemma. In today's youth sport landscape, parents face enormous social and cultural pressures to provide their children with every possible resource to succeed. The fear of missing out (FOMO) on potential opportunities drives many parents to go to great lengths to ensure their children have access to the best possible development environments. An extension of the FOMO phenomenon is Fear of My Child Missing Out. FO(my child!)MO amplifies the pressure parents experience worrying that if their child doesn't participate in the intense training and competition, they will fall behind or miss out on opportunities. The pull towards elitism and social exclusivity of high-end training programs, along with the social capital of being a successful athletic family, adds another layer of pressure. Social media can exacerbate this pressure, where parents can see curated images and stories of other children's successes, adding to the pressure to push their own child to excel. As Theodore Roosevelt said: "*comparison is the thief of joy*", and parents caught in the cycle of comparing their child's performance—or their performance as parents—to others, can create a great deal of anxiety.

It cannot be ignored that some parents' own motivations and desires influence the decisions made around a child's sporting experience. Often, these motivations stem from parents' personal psychology, such as past experiences, unfulfilled ambitions, unresolved relational trauma, and self-identity. When parents have unresolved issues or unmet needs from their own development, they may project these onto their children. This can manifest as pushing their children towards specific goals or activities that align more with the parent's past desires than the child's current interests. In youth sport, this projection can lead to a child being pressured to excel in a sport that the parent once aspired to succeed in or was never given the chance to pursue. The parent's happiness and sense of accomplishment become tied to the child's achievements, creating a high-pressure environment where the child feels responsible for fulfilling their parent's dreams.

These projections are often unconscious, meaning parents may not realize they are imposing their past desires onto their children. But the consequences can be very real. Children may struggle with feelings of inadequacy, anxiety, and pressure to meet unrealistic expectations. Furthermore, when a child does not share the same level of investment or interest in the athletic opportunities created for them by their parent(s), it can lead to feelings of resentment towards the child. Parents may feel unappreciated or frustrated that their sacrifices and efforts are not yielding the expected enthusiasm or success from their child, leading to significant relational strain.

Identifying how parents' psychology impacts their children's sporting decisions is not about shaming or placing blame. Instead, it's about fostering understanding and empathy for how reasonable people can sometimes make unreasonable demands and irrational choices that do not align with their long-term goals for their children.

This awareness is crucial because it highlights how deeply ingrained motivations, desires, and past experiences can influence behavior, often without conscious realization.

With awareness and understanding, parents can begin to recognize patterns in their decision-making that may not serve their child's best interests. This newfound awareness empowers parents to make decisions that are more aligned with their true goals of fostering a healthy, balanced, and fulfilling sporting experience for their child.

With choice comes freedom. When parents understand the psychological underpinnings of their actions, they can break free from the cycle of pressure and anxiety that often accompanies youth sports. They can prioritize their child's well-being, enjoy the journey alongside them, and support their development in a way that honors their child's individuality.

Ultimately, sport is about creating a positive and enriching environment where children can thrive, develop resilience, and find joy in their activities, knowing that their parents are fully behind them, grounded in love and understanding.

The next section introduces a strategy and challenge for parents to do just that.

Unlocking the Developmental Dilemma

Parenting a young athlete in today's youth sports landscape is a daunting task. The pressure to ensure a child's success can easily pull parents into the relentless 'arms race', where the fear of missing out drives them to seek every possible advantage for their children. However, research on early specialization indicates that doing so does not necessarily increase the chances of reaching elite levels and may even introduce several potential negative physical, social, and psychological challenges.

So, what are parents to do? The developmental dilemma places parents in a bind: investing in early development and providing the most competitive and enriched sporting environment seems necessary to keep up with the best players but carries limited return on investment and significant risks. On the other hand, prioritizing a healthier development with diverse experiences promotes the growth of a well-rounded child but may feel like it undermines the chance for their child to excel in a sport they love.

There is no easy answer. There is no algorithm that will tell parents the correct developmental path for their child. There is no crystal ball. Sorry to disappoint. But there is hope—parents who are clear on their role and focused on the most important aspects of their child's sporting journey will navigate the challenges of youth sport with clarity, conviction, and empowerment.

To do this, the mindset of many parents must shift. Parents must be unbound by the distorted beliefs of early specialization, winning as the sole measure of success, and the notion that they are responsible for creating the athletic potential of their children. They must unburden themselves from the pressure and conflict they feel, and ensure their child has a positive and healthy experience, regardless of their level or potential.

> *"If your child is meant to, they will make it."*

This is it. This is the reality that is the key to easing the pressure of the developmental dilemma. Let it sink in. Read it again. Within this statement is a liberating truth for sports parents. It means that a child's innate characteristics, talents, and abilities, guided by the grace of God, will be the primary determinants of their athletic success and level of achievement. It means that athletic success will actualize naturally through the child. It means that the world will find a gifted athlete, not the other way around.

The statement *"if your child is meant to, they will make it"* recognizes that while parents do provide support and opportunities, they cannot control every outcome. A child's athletic success will be the result of their intrinsic qualities that will naturally come to the forefront if a child is meant to excel. Every child possesses a unique set of innate abilities and characteristics that contribute to their potential. These inherent qualities provide the foundation for their athletic development. While early specialization and enriched environments can nurture and refine these qualities, they do not magically create new potential.

Too simple, you might say? *"This reality isn't realistic at all! It doesn't account for any of the external factors that contribute to an athlete's success."* Yes, that's true. And that is by design. While the position that *"if your child is meant to, they will make it"* may seem to oversimplify the complexities of sports success, it pointedly recognizes that much of those circumstances are out of a parent's and child's control. It does not dismiss the fact that there are many factors that can make a difference in an athlete's trajectory: genetics, special coaches, team dynamics, opportunity, timing, and commitment—all of which are integral to capitalizing on athletic potential. While these environmental factors can provide valuable opportunities for growth and development, it is essential to recognize that they work *with* a child's inherent potential—they do not increase it.

A child's inherent athletic potential will always outperform its environment.

The point of this mindset is not to dismiss the importance of other factors, but to help parents shift their focus away from trying to control every aspect of their child's athletic journey and instead, focus on supporting their child's development and enjoyment of the sport. While parents can certainly provide opportunities for their child to succeed, that success is not solely determined by these external factors. Parents who can adopt this reality and let go of the constant pressure to seek out new opportunities, can instead focus on nurturing their child's natural abilities and passion for the sport as it reveals itself.

Yes, enriched environments and early specialization lead children to higher levels of achievement faster. But the research on early sport specialization shows that sped up youth development is a false indicator of potential for long-term sporting success. Early levels of achievement show early mastery—and that's all.

In reality, children who achieve elite athletic status at an early age rarely end up being the most successful. It is athletes who continuously improve and elevate their abilities, skills, and performance over time are the ones who achieve the longest career in sport. The fact is athletes that play at the highest levels aren't always the best players at every level they play at. They simply have a longer developmental trajectory—they just keep improving. This means that parents don't have to rush their child into early specialization and worry about them being left behind. If they have the talent, innate characteristics, and potential, they will catch up quickly—even leaving the rest of the pack in their dust.

Early experiences and enriched environments help actualize potential, but they do not increase potential

---

Qualifier Statement on Early Specialization!

The mindset of *"if your child is meant to, they will make it"* is not about dismissing early specialization; it's about aligning parents' decision-making and priorities around shaping the most beneficial sports journey for their child rather than trying to secure the destination of athletic success. In sports like gymnastics or swimming, where athletes often reach their peak in adolescence, early specialization is not just beneficial—it's necessary. However, it's critically important that this path is chosen because it aligns with a child's enthusiasm and a family's priorities, not because parents feel forced into it by external pressures. There's absolutely nothing wrong with early specialization when it's a choice made from a genuine desire to pursue excellence in a specific sport. And early specialization must be kept healthy: even if your child plays at the highest levels, parents must remember that their well-being and holistic development should never be compromised for the sake of athletic achievement. If a child is meant to achieve greatness, they will, and this will be because they found joy and fulfillment in their journey, not because they sacrificed their best life to chase a singular goal.

Accepting this reality that *"if your child is meant to, they will make it"* can be life changing. It will unlock the anxieties of the developmental dilemma and return the ability to make choices that are best for a child's athletic and holistic well-being without guilt, fear, shame, excessive pride, or selfishness. It will create the opportunity to experience joy with your child and fully embrace the gift of youth sport and leverage all it offers. *"If your child is meant to, they will make it"* creates space for parents to embrace the joy of watching their child grow and develop through sports and trust that they will find their path, whatever that may be— and let the rest take care of itself.

What if I Completely Disagree with *"if your child is meant to, they will make it?"*

You may not believe the statement *"if your child is meant to, they will make it."* You may think that you have evidence and experiences to the contrary. Many parents, coaches, and athletes could make an argument that *"if your child is meant to, they will make it"* is inaccurate. They may argue that it was the unique opportunities, coaching experiences, and access to development that allowed certain athletes to reach their fullest potential. It is certainly reasonable to acknowledge these factors and how they could have played a significant role in an athlete's success. *"If your child is meant to, they will make it"* isn't meant to explain every athletic success story. However, it does offer a chance for every athletic story to be successful.

"If your child is meant to, they will make it" might be a difficult pill to swallow for many parents. Some parents want to believe they can transform their child into a star. But the reality is a child's innate abilities and characteristics will primarily determine their athletic trajectory, regardless of how much effort or resources parents invest in their development. And if a parent can accept this, it can be incredibly liberating.

What "*if your child is meant to, they will make it*" Is Not

Believing in the reality of *"if your child is meant to, they will make it"* does not imply that sport parenting should be passive, or that there is nothing parents can do to support their child's athletic journey. On the contrary, it requires an active and intentional approach, one that may involve significant sacrifices and commitments. Parents will still find themselves dedicating weekends, working overtime, and sacrificing personal time and date nights to support their child's sporting activities. The key difference lies in the motivations behind these sacrifices. Adopting the mindset of *"if your child is meant to, they will make it"* significantly changes the motivational context of the sacrifices families make for sports. When parents embrace this reality, they no longer feel held hostage to the belief that they must do everything possible to ensure their child's athletic success. Instead, sacrifices such as spending weekends at tournaments, working overtime to afford training, or giving up personal time become conscious, deliberate choices made with a focus on the collective well-being of the child and the family. They reinforce family and personal values and are seen as important to the growth and development for both parents and children. These decisions are evaluated for their overall benefit, ensuring that they align with the child's natural interests and abilities, and contribute to a positive family experience.

"If your child is meant to, they will make it" is not to say that the child always rules or that this mindset is allowing a child to take the path of least resistance. Within the *"if your child is meant to, they will make it"* mindset of parents, it is still critical that parents hold children accountable to ensure their efforts and actions are aligned with their commitments and goals. Yet in this mindset, the tone of the accountability is grounded in compassion and support rather than guilt and pressure. Rather than using threats or guilt to enforce standards or expectations, a parent's call for accountability can be about providing foresight and perspective.

Even if you don't fully believe the reality that *"if your child is meant to, they will make it,"* adopting and living it will make the sporting experience more enjoyable for you and your child.

In the next section explores what a *"if your child is meant to, they will make it"* mindset can unlock for parents willing to take the leap.

Benefits of Adopting
"If your Child is meant to, they will make it"
Mindset

"If your child is meant to, they will make it" can be seen as a
key, unlocking many of the challenges that contribute to
the developmental dilemma. It can serve to focus parent's
attention and support them to withstand the pressures of
the youth sports landscape, allowing them truly use sport
as a development tool in their child's life.

Unlock #1: It Unburdens Parents

The belief that *"if your child is meant to, they will make it"* reduces the burden on parents to provide all the resources for their child's athletic development. If a child's potential is innate and will naturally self-actualize through their unique lived experience, then parents can recalibrate how much difference they think they can make in their child's developmental journey. From this position, more does not always mean more.

This perspective can ease the immense pressure parents often feel to orchestrate every aspect of their child's sports journey. It releases the burden of feeling solely responsible for their child's success and opens a space for a more balanced and enjoyable sports experience. Parents can focus on providing support, guidance, and a nurturing environment while trusting in their child's abilities to navigate their own path.

Early specialization and intense competitive development programs make it easy to get caught up and focused on their child playing on the best team in the best league at every level to ensure their success. Adopting this mindset helps parents ease pressure on themselves and their children, allowing them to create distance from the obligation and control over their child's success. Afterall, if the child is meant to, they will make it! By accepting this reality, parents can relax and focus on the areas that provide support and guidance instead of trying to control every aspect of their child's athletic development. Oh, what a relief!

Unlock # 2: It Keeps FO(my child!)MO in Check

Parents often feel immense pressure to ensure their child is on the "right" team, attending the "right" tournaments, and playing with the "right" coaches. This fear of missing out (FO(my child!)MO) can be overwhelming, leading to a constant state of stress and anxiety. The mindset that *"if your child is meant to, they will make it"* can significantly ease parents' FO(my child!)MO, offering relief from the relentless pursuit of every possible opportunity to increase their child's potential.

The social pressures driving FO(my child!)MO are pervasive. Parents see other children excelling, hear stories of their early achievements, and witness the accolades and attention other children receive and other parents boast of. This can create a sense of urgency and competition, compelling parents to invest heavily in specialized coaching, exclusive teams, and intensive training programs. Social media amplifies this pressure by showcasing the successes of other children, making it easy for parents to compare their own child's progress unfavorably. The constant comparison and fear of falling behind can lead to decisions driven more by anxiety than by what is genuinely best for the child.

Adopting the mindset that *"if your child is meant to, they will make it"* helps to alleviate these pressures. It shifts the focus from external validation and societal benchmarks to an appreciation of each child's unique journey. This belief encourages parents to trust in their child's inherent potential and individual path, reducing the compulsion to chase every opportunity for fear of missing out. By recognizing that every child has their own timeline and set of opportunities, parents can find peace in supporting their child's development without succumbing to the pressure of constant comparison.

A Word About "Trust the Process" and the "Process Paradox"

The adage "trust the process" has become a common sports aphorism that emphasizes the importance of focusing on the journey rather than solely on the result. It suggests that success is not only determined by outcomes but by a commitment to a systematic approach to development and growth. This mindset recognizes that success is largely determined by several uncontrollable factors and therefore, one's attention and effort should be focused on the things that are in one's control—the process.

Trust the process regularly adopted and spoken of at the highest levels of sport, especially professional athletics. It is common to hear elite and professional coaches and players in their press conferences talk about implementing a strategy that trusts the process. Posted in locker rooms are phrases and quotes reminding players that process is key to success. The point is this: At the highest levels of sport competition—where only results matter—athletes and teams entirely emphasize the importance of the process. It would seem that there is a process paradox—the higher the stakes become; the less athletes focus on results.

Professional athletes and successful organizations attribute their success to the incremental processes that were adhered to along the way. Success is not an outcome, it's the product of habit. They understand that by focusing on day-to-day improvements, refining skills, and building a strong foundation, they increase their chances of long-term success, even when many contributing factors are uncontrollable. Nick Saban—winner of 7 national college football titles has been quoted saying this about the process: *"Don't think about winning the SEC Championship. Don't think about the national championship. Think about what you needed to do in this drill, on this play, in this moment. That's the process: Let's think about what we can do today, the task at hand."*

Compare that with youth sports, where results have little to no long-term significance, yet there is an excessive emphasis on winning and performance as measures of success. Parents, coaches, and even young athletes often fixate on winning and performance, which can hinder their ability to fully embrace the process of skill development, learning, and overall growth.

The process paradox highlights how backwards the priorities of youth sport can be. By shifting the focus from immediate outcomes to appreciating the journey of improvement and development, parents put their children in a better position on and off the field because they are focused on shaping the process rather than being the arbiter of performance and success. If the competitors at the highest professional levels practice a mindset that shifts away from outcomes as determinants of success, surely parents in youth sports can too.

Unlock #3: Focus can Shift to the Process

"If your child is meant to, they will make it" is a mindset that trusts the process. This perspective encourages parents to focus on the day-to-day efforts and habits that contribute to long-term development. By emphasizing these elements, parents can help their children build a solid foundation in their sport, ensuring that their progress is steady and sustainable. Without sustained interest and passion for the sport, no amount of skill development and access to resources is going to produce any long-term results anyway. Without a love of process, no athlete will be successful. Not only trusting—but loving— the process is critical for long-term success.

"If your child is meant to, they will make it" allows parents and children to appreciate incremental gains by encouraging a process-focused perspective. This helps children and parents stay within what they can control:

effort, attitude, and commitment rather than becoming fixated on external outcomes like winning or losing, which are often beyond their control.

Unlock #4: It Helps Parents Reshape Goal Setting

Sport can be a difficult place to learn to set meaningful and achievable goals. Because of the intense focus on winning, process-oriented goals are often disregarded in favor of aspirations that individuals may have little control over. *"Winning a championship"* or *"playing Division I"*, for example, are not goals—they are aspirations.

Most think that they need to set their goals on the highest possible accomplishments to achieve their fullest potential and vision of success in sport. Further to that point, many think that setting lower, more realistic goals is hedging your bets, aiming too low, or compromising your intentions to protect yourself from failure. While both have grains of truth, they are both flawed — You must dream big, but you must plan small.

"If your child is meant to, they will make it" helps parents shift their child's attention away from the need to only

focus on aspirations. This mindset believes that aspirations will take care of themselves, allowing parents to direct their children to focus on the process and the present. It relieves the pressure to singular aspirations by emphasizing the importance of incremental gains, quality preparation, and staying within what they can control. With this perspective, parents can rest easy, knowing that if their child is engaged, passionate, and consistently working towards their goals, the larger aspirations will naturally align with what the world holds for them. This mindset promotes a healthy and positive sporting experience, where the journey is valued as much as the destination because the goals reflect value in the journey, not just the destination.

Unlock #5: It Creates an Opportunity to Prioritize Fun

In the professionalized world of youth sports, there is an overwhelming emphasis on performance and being "good' over having fun. The achievement-focused ethos of youth sport projects the belief that things are more fun when you're good at them—a half truth. Demonstrating competence in any task is enjoyable, but when the emphasis is solely on "being good" or improving skills, the pressure to perform can overshadow the pleasure of the activity itself. Therefore, it is important to recognize that being good at a sport and enjoying it are related but two separate things. When an activity is fun, it is an enjoyable experience regardless of the outcome. It's not about winning or losing or getting better—but exploring, learning and having a good time. It's important to encourage children to have fun playing, regardless of their performance.

The mindset *"if your child is meant to, they will make it"* prioritizes fun by alleviating the pressure to excel all the time—the child will become who they were born to be regardless of their performance in any one practice, game, or skill session. Parents can shift their focus from the need for constant progression and performance to creating opportunities for actual fun. Instead of solely focusing on the mechanics, skills, and providing constructive feedback, there is an opportunity to play, joke around, laugh, and even be silly. *"If your child is meant to, they will make it"* reminds parents that sport will always be a child's game and is best experienced under the conditions of fun, which is a quality that parents can play an important role in creating for their child.

Unlock #6: It Reframes "Quitting"

In the world of youth sports, quitting and moving on from a sport are often conflated. Quitting implies giving up or abandoning something without reason or cause. It suggests a lack of perseverance and a failure to see things through to the end. Quitting is reneging on a commitment. It is very different from a child and their family deciding to move away from a previously fulfilled commitment and consider other passions and areas of interest. In every sport, athletes who fulfill their commitments and then decide to move onto something else are labeled as quitters. *"He quit the sport," "she quit the team"* are common attributions.

The mindset *"if your child is meant to, they will make it"* can change how parents frame quitting and moving on. Parents often resist supporting their child's desire to move on due to the fear that their child is giving up on their potential. However, embracing this mindset means accepting that if a child is truly passionate and talented, they will find their way back to the sport, regardless of momentary changes in direction. Quitting implies failure, and in many cases, when a child's interest or ability to play competitive sports is at an end, they are anything but failures. So why frame their experience that way?

In youth sports, there are many valid reasons a child may want to move on. Perhaps they've lost interest in the sport, or they've discovered a new passion that they want to pursue. Maybe the coaching style or team dynamics aren't a good fit for them, or they're experiencing physical or emotional burnout. Whatever the reason, it's important for parents to listen to their children and support them in deciding what's right for them. When a child moves on from a sport, it's not a failure or a reflection of their character. It's simply a natural part of the growth process.

This is not to say that there aren't situations where parents encourage children to stick with a sport, even if they're not enjoying it in the moment. Motivating them to honor their commitments is often necessary—great sports parents don't let their kids off the hook. Yet the mindset "*if your child is meant to, they will make it*" helps parents to more accurately see that moving on is not quitting but may actually be part of a healthy developmental process. It can create space to reflect on the initial goals and outcomes that drove parents and children to sport in the first place and give perspective to consider what's best for the child's development and experience.

Unlock #7: It Keeps Vicarious Living in Check

Living vicariously through children is an expression used to describe the phenomenon of excessively experiencing life through their experiences, achievements, and challenges. Youth sports is a common arena for living vicariously through children, often manifesting as parents becoming deeply invested in their child's athletic pursuits. Parents may feel pride in their child's successes as if they were their own or experience disappointment in their child's failures on a personal level. While this can be natural and even beneficial when done in a healthy manner, it can also lead to negative outcomes if the boundaries between the parent's and child's experiences become blurred.

The mindset of *"if your child is meant to, they will make it"* helps parents live vicariously through their children in a healthy way. It reinforces a perspective where parents can share in their children's joys and achievements without over-investing. This is because *"if your child is meant to, they will make it"* acknowledges that a child's sports journey is personal to them. It encourages parents to passively share in their child's success, understanding that the accomplishments and achievements ultimately belong to the child. The same goes for a child's failure—parents can feel with and for their child's struggles but still maintain a distance to recognize that it is their child's battle and not theirs.

Healthy vicarious *experiencing* involves sharing in the emotions associated with a child's successes and failures while recognizing that their journey is separate from one's own. This is a state where parents provide support and encouragement without losing sight of their own identities and aspirations. In contrast, unhealthy vicarious *living* occurs when parents become overly invested in their child's pursuits, tying their self-worth and identity too closely to their child's achievements. This can lead to undue pressure on the child and strain the parent-child relationship.

To determine if you are excessively invested in your child's sports experience, analyze your emotional reactions to your child's successes and failures. Excessive celebration, devastation or anxiety over your child's performance or porting circumstances may indicate overinvestment. Parental behavior at the field or during competitions can be a particularly revealing indicator. Excessive shouting from the sidelines, arguing with referees, engaging in confrontations with other parents, and heaving criticism of other players usually suggests that a parent is too emotionally entangled in their child's sports journey.

"If your child is meant to, they will make it," provides parents instant perspective. This mindset does not need a child to win every game or for refs to get every call right to fully realize their athletic potential—it has a relaxing effect on parental participation. Through *"if your child is meant to, they will make it"* parents can focus their energy and

enthusiasm to where their child needs it most—

encouragement and support.

Unlock #8: It Creates an Opportunity to Reframe "Bad Coaches"

Let's face it: not every team or coach that a child plays for will be God's gift to coaching and athlete development. Believing that *"if my child is meant to, they will make it"* gives a chance to reframe negative coaching or team experiences in a child's sports journey.

Nothing can be harder on a parent than watching their child experience a difficult learning and playing environment. It's hard to resist the urge to rescue those children from their situation, ensuring their safety, well-being, and giving them the opportunities they deserve. This reaction is further exacerbated by a myth of the developmental dilemma that says if a child is not getting peak performance and peak conditions at every level, they will fall behind. *"If your child is meant to, they will make it"* creates space to reconsider the knee-jerk reaction to pull a child out of a tough environment. It allows parents and children to reframe these experiences and recognize that they could be meaningful development opportunities that contribute to resilience, self-reliance, and self-confidence.

It is understandable to feel frustrated or upset when a child is faced with unfavorable coaching situations or unfair playing time, but these can be opportunities for growth. Rather than immediately seeking to rectify the situation or remove the child from the team, parents can choose to embrace these challenges as teaching moments.

One of the ways parents can do this is by encouraging their child to find the gift in difficult situations. This is a critical lesson and experience for children who will—at some point in their life— find themselves in a situation where others do not recognize their potential or worth. This may happen in the classroom or in a job. Sport provides parents and children with challenging experiences that lead to personal growth, character building, and perspective. It may be natural to want to remove a child from a difficult coach or suboptimal team but consider *"if your child is meant to, they will make it"*, and this experience—even though it feels negative in the moment—can play an important role in their development.

It is important to note that this perspective does not excuse inappropriate or abusive behavior by coaches. Parents should be vigilant in distinguishing between sub-optimal coaching and abusive coaching, ensuring the safety and well-being of their child.

The mindset *"if your child is meant to, they will make it"* gives parents perspective to let children endure difficult situations. In doing so, children are empowered to make choices on how they interpret and respond to their environment, cultivating resilience and character, helping them grow as athletes and people.

Closing the Loop

Adopting the mindset of *"if your child is meant to, they will make it"* can significantly alleviate the pressures and challenges sport parents often experience. By embracing this mindset, parents can reduce the overwhelming need to provide every possible resource for their child's athletic development and instead, focus on offering support and guidance without micromanaging.

The fear of missing out on potential opportunities often drives parents to make hasty decisions, leading to stress and anxiety. The mindset that *"if your child is meant to, they will make it"* helps alleviate this fear by shifting the focus from external validation to appreciating each child's unique journey. By trusting that their child will find their way, parents can create a more supportive environment that prioritizes their child's love for the sport and personal growth over competitive milestones.

Embracing this mindset also shifts the emphasis from outcomes to the process of growth and development. Parents can focus on the day-to-day efforts and habits that contribute to long-term development, such as incremental gains, quality preparation, and staying within one's control. This approach not only alleviates pressure but also nurtures a child's intrinsic motivation to improve and enjoy the sport.

The mindset *"if your child is meant to, they will make it"* reminds parents that sports are best experienced under conditions of fun, which they can significantly influence. It also removes the fear that moving on from a sport equates to giving up or leaving unrealized potential on the table.

The potential upside in adopting *"if your child is meant to, they will make it"* as a mindset is enormous—greater family harmony, a more supportive environment for your child, and an overall more rewarding and enjoyable experience. Make the commitment to try this approach for just one season, and you might find that it not only benefits your child's development but also enriches your entire family's experience with youth sport.

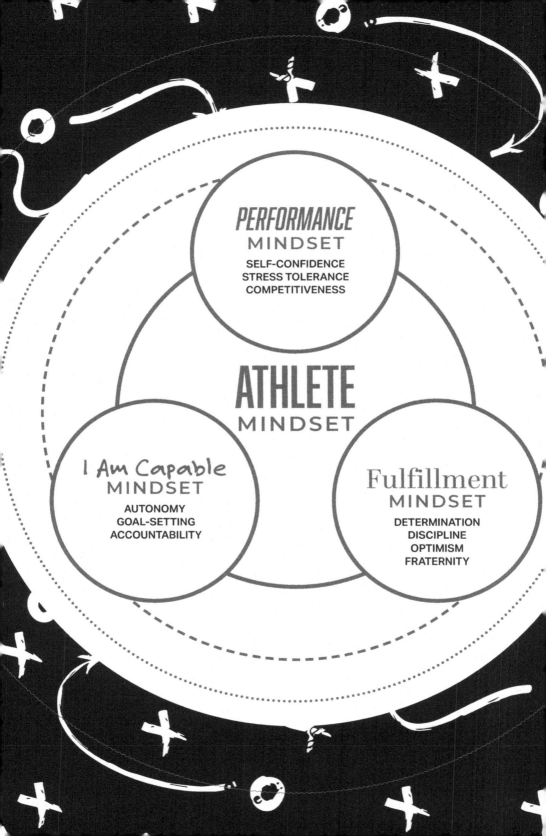

The Athlete Mindset

Adopting the mindset " *if your child is meant to, they will make it"* unburdens parents of unnecessary responsibility, allowing them to experience less FO(my child)MO, be more supportive, and enjoy their child's sports journey to the fullest regardless of their level of success. But *"if my child is meant to, they will make it"* does not mean that parents should simply be passive spectators. Rather, it encourages parents to refocus and actively contribute to the most productive, healthy, and long-lasting aspects of their children's sporting journey.

Parents require a straightforward reference point to ensure that their child's athletic experiences, regardless of the level, align with their overall development. By utilizing the *Athletic Mindset* as a guide, parents can ensure their child's sports experience does just that.

The *Athlete Mindset* is a model designed to promote both athletic and personal success in young athletes. It was created to be a barometer for parents to ensure that their child's sporting experience is making a positive developmental impact—if a child is experiencing an opportunity to build out the *Athlete Mindset*, then their athletic experience is doing its job regardless of the level they play at or achieve.

The *Athlete Mindset* is built upon three core pillars: the Performance Mindset, the 'I Am Capable' Mindset, and the Fulfillment Mindset. Each Mindset is the summation of a set of unique behavioral characteristics that work together to position children to be successful not only in sports but in all facets of life.

The Performance Mindset emphasizes self-confidence, stress management, and competitiveness. This mindset cultivates young athletes to approach high-pressure situations with a focus on execution. The 'I Am Capable' Mindset focuses on self-efficacy and personal growth. This mindset facilitates a strong sense of autonomy, accountability, and a proactive approach to setting and achieving goals. It encourages athletes to believe in their ability to learn and improve continually through inner strength and agency. Finally, the Fulfillment Mindset manifests in the form of determination, discipline, optimism, and fraternity. It is a mindset that drives athletes and individuals to maintain a positive outlook in the face of setbacks, set strong personal values, and invest in relationships to reach their goals. It underscores the importance of finding satisfaction and joy in the journey of personal and athletic development—even when it sucks. Together, these mindsets form a holistic approach to nurturing young athletes, preparing them for success in sports and beyond.

Cultivating an *Athletic Mindset* in alignment with a *"if my child is meant to, they will make it"* attitude, both parents and children can experience empowerment, purpose, and joy through youth sports.

All Levels of Competition Can Develop the Athlete Mindset

The *Athlete Mindset* is applicable to all athletic experiences no matter what level of competition a child is participating in. For those children competing at the highest levels, the *Athlete Mindset* can help parents ensure their child's development is not compromised for athletic success. The *Athlete Mindset* can also be fully cultivated and expressed in less competitive sporting environments. The *Athletic Mindset* is a reference to ensure a child is getting a healthy and valuable sports development experience.

The *Athlete Mindset* is the practical embodiment of the belief that *"if a child is meant to, they will make it."* It acknowledges the innate potential of each child, while guiding parents to foster the mindsets, values, and skills

that will serve their children to reach their unique

individual potential in and out of sport.

The Performance Mindset

Performance is an essential aspect of life. To succeed, one must be able to perform under stress. In many cases, successful individuals have the ability to 'rise to the occasion', not letting the significance or pressure of the situation impact their capabilities. Rather than being intimidated by the high stakes of win-or-lose scenarios, they see a chance to showcase their skills, demonstrate their potential, and achieve their goals. The capacity to embrace the opportunity to excel and succeed, even in the face of competition and pressure, reflects a Performance Mindset.

Getting children comfortable with performing under pressure is a necessary aspect of development. From the classroom to the sports arena, to the college application process, to the job market—how one performs under conditions of competition plays a big role in the outcome. Allowing children to experience the nature of competition and cultivating their capacity to perform prepares them for a competitive world.

Sport can be a great way to cultivate a Performance Mindset in children. It provides a controlled environment where children can experience stress and learn to manage it effectively. With the right instruction and guidance, children can view these high-pressure situations as opportunities to show excellence rather than fearing failure. Most importantly, sport encourages children to compete against others, teaching them to be motivated rather than intimidated by those who are trying to achieve the same goals as they are.

Self-Confidence

Self-confidence is a key factor in developing a Performance Mindset. Confident individuals possess an inner self-assurance that their goals are within their grasp and trust their own judgment. They are also less likely to let setbacks affect their perception of what they are capable of—confidence fuels healthy risk taking.

Sport is a fantastic way to build self-confidence in children. Sport puts difficult skills and performance conditions between children and their goals. When they can work through those conditions to reach their goals, there is an opportunity for self-confidence to blossom. This can lead to a positive feedback loop where the more they take on new challenges, the more confident they become to push themselves further.

Sport can also create conditions for self-confidence development by challenging children to stick with 'hard things.' For example, if a child is struggling to learn a new skill, they may fail multiple times before finally getting it right. This can be frustrating, but when children see they can keep trying and eventually succeed, their confidence grows, and they learn that failure is a natural part of the learning process—not a reflection of their overall capability. As a result, children can develop a positive self-image and the belief that they can achieve great things in sport and in other areas of their life even if they experience failures and setbacks.

Being a part of a team can also boost a child's confidence. When children feel like they belong to a group and receive appreciation for their contributions, it is more likely that they will feel confident in themselves and their abilities. Parents can play an important role in ensuring sporting opportunities contribute to the development of self-confidence and a positive self-image.

Here are some key approaches to fostering confidence in young athletes:

Acknowledge Steps Toward Mastery

Acknowledging a child's steps toward mastery is an effective way to build self-confidence. When parents recognize the effort and strategies their children employ to improve, it shifts the focus from their innate abilities to appreciating the power of their hard work. Instead of wondering, *"Am I good enough?"* children begin to think, *"If I work hard enough, I am capable of doing this."* This approach helps them understand that mastery is not about innate talent but about the cumulative effect of the effort they put into their journey.

One effective technique to foster confidence is to focus on specifically on effort and improvements rather than just their success. This is a commonly cited strategy, and for good reason: when feedback is solely focused on the results, children might interpret this as a judgment on their overall capability. When feedback is focused on effort, a child's capabilities are associated with the acknowledgment of sustained effort rather than success or lack thereof.

Do I recognize and praise my child's effort during practices and games, even when they don't win, rather than just focusing on their victories or pointing out their mistakes?

By recognizing the hard work and associating it with the progress a child makes, parents reinforce the value of effort and persistence, naturally elevating their confidence by increasing their willingness to sustain effort. Children must not only be confident that they can be successful, but also have the confidence that their sustained effort will produce the results they desire. Celebrating incremental gains may seem small but have can have a big impact on how a child perceives their capabilities.

How often do I take the time to celebrate my effort?

Expanding the Comfort Zone

Fostering a supportive environment where children feel safe to take risks and step outside their comfort zones is essential to developing self-confidence. Specifically, trying new things and having an openness to take risks are validate and reinforce healthy self-beliefs about one's capability. Parents play an important role in orienting their children to try new things and push themselves. Learning new skills, trying new sports or trying out for new teams, and playing against different groups can create an environment that exposes children to taking risks and becoming more comfortable with testing their capabilities. This also extends to social situations—encouraging children to put themselves out there to meet new people, foster friendships, and build social skills.

Expanding a child's comfort zone is only effective if there is a meaningful reflection period for the child to consider how they 'thought' it would go versus how it actually went. This may reveal self-limiting beliefs or doubts that your child holds about their capabilities in new situations. Use the opportunity to reinforce and praise a child's willingness to try and how their new experience gives new evidence to reframe some of those previously held beliefs. This can greatly impact their self-perception and shape their willingness to try new things in the future.

When children internalize this message, they become confident and willing to take on challenges. They know that their hard work plays a big role in what they are capable of, which in turn, expands what they think they are capable of.

Stress Tolerance

Stress is an inevitable part of life and those who can manage stress effectively are better equipped to handle life's challenges. Learning how to tolerate stress is an essential skill that supports performing under pressure. Developing stress tolerance is needed for a child's healthy development as it prepares them to cope with the demands of daily life. Effective stress management skills enable children to develop a sense of control over their emotions and thoughts, which supports a Performance Mindset.

Sport provides a unique opportunity for children to experience and learn to manage stress in a controlled and safe environment. In sport, stress can arise from various situations such as competition, game pressure, making choices, setting goals, and time management. Through regular participation, children can become accustomed to higher-pressure situations and learn how to handle them effectively. They can learn to identify their triggers, develop positive self-talk, and techniques to manage uncertainty and changing circumstances. Parents can play a role in helping children learn to manage their stress by providing support and guidance during challenging times. By learning to manage stress in a controlled environment like sport, children can develop the ability to adapt to stressful situations in other areas of their lives.

Consider these approaches to fostering stress tolerance in young athletes:

KYC! (Know your Child!)

Understanding and recognizing a child's unique stress patterns is imperative. Every child handles stress differently, and it's important to respect these differences. Some children may thrive under pressure, while others might need a more supportive approach to build their stress tolerance. Parents can help children identify stress triggers and develop strategies to manage them.

*How well do I know my child's stress
response patterns?*

By observing how children perceive and respond to
stressful situations, parents can help them acclimate to the
pressures effectively. This involves recognizing the signs
of stress in their child such as changes in behavior, mood,
or physical symptoms. Parents can ask probing questions
like: *"I noticed that you get really emotional in stressful
situations, what are some of the thoughts you are thinking
through those times?"* This line of questioning can help
parents understand how children are perceiving stressful
situations and what might be impacting their ability to
navigate it effectively, guiding parents to better
understand their child's experience.

Understanding how your child processes and reacts to
stress is an essential part of ensuring they are operating
within optimal stress levels—those that challenge them to
grow without overwhelming them. By using your
observations and engaging in open dialogue, parents can

gauge whether their child is navigating stress in a way that builds resilience or if they are experiencing distress that exceeds their current coping resources. This approach allows you to fine-tune their exposure to challenging situations, ensuring they are developmentally ready for the pressures they face. When parents are attuned to their child's stress signals and adjust accordingly, they can create an environment where their child feels supported and capable, yet still fostering a Performance Mindset.

Call it By Name

Helping children identify and label what is causing them stress can be a powerful tool in managing and overcoming it. By 'calling it by name,' children can better understand their stressors, recognize their temporary nature, and seek solutions rather than succumbing to self-limiting thoughts or beliefs. This approach encourages children to focus on specific aspects of the stressful situation, which can make the stress feel more manageable and less overwhelming.

Encourage your child to articulate what exactly is causing their stress. Ask probing questions like: *Can you tell me what specifically makes you feel anxious or stressed during games or practices?* By labeling the stressor—whether it's the fear of making mistakes, pressure from competition, or worries about letting the team down—children can start to see these issues as specific challenges rather than insurmountable obstacles. This helps them shift their focus from anxiety to actionable steps they can take to address the problem. This shift supports their ability to perform well despite the stressful circumstances.

Just Breathe

Sharing de-stressing activities with your child, such as mindful breathing exercises or other self-regulation strategies, can significantly enhance their ability to manage stress. Focusing on the breath is key to activating the parasympathetic nervous system, which promotes relaxation and calmness, essential for performing tasks under pressure. Many people do not realize that breathing is a skill that requires practice and teaching children this skill can equip them with a powerful tool to manage stress and improve performance in sports and other areas of life.

Incorporating breathing techniques during sporting events helps children regulate their emotions and stay present. Encourage your child to take deep, calming breaths before a big game or during breaks to reset their focus and reduce anxiety. This can help children make the connection between their breath and their performance. This recognition can motivate them to incorporate these techniques independently, enhancing their ability to manage stress and perform well under pressure.

Do I encourage and participate in strategies and techniques to de-stress with my child?

Making breathing exercises a routine part of your child's preparation for sporting events helps reinforce its importance. Reflecting on the in-sport benefits can help solidify this practice as a key part of their stress management toolkit.

Competitiveness

Competition is an inescapable reality of life. From the earliest age, there is competition for attention, affection, and resources. A Performance Mindset relies heavily on the ability to thrive in competitive situations. Children who thrive in win or lose scenarios and compete in a healthy way are better equipped to face life's challenges.

Sport provides a natural arena for children to develop their ability to thrive in competitive scenarios. Sport exposes children to face situations where they must compete with their peers and *practice* winning and losing. Children develop a sense of what it takes to win, how to process a loss, and most importantly, how to adapt to each outcome.

Here are a few strategies to enhance your child's motivational orientation to be competitive through sport:

Facing and Overcoming Fear

 One of the hardest things to do is to step into the proverbial ring and give it your best shot, knowing that someone else may be better. This fear is a natural part of competition that must be overcome to be effective. This can only be done by looking fear in the face and becoming comfortable with it.

Do I help my child pinpoint what they're afraid of when it comes to competitive situations and let them face and overcome those fears?

By acknowledging the fear, children can start to understand its origins and evaluate whether it's based on real threats or irrational thoughts. This process helps demystify fear and reduces its power, allowing children to focus on their performance rather than being paralyzed by anxiety.

This encouragement helps children see fear as a challenge to be met rather than an obstacle to avoid. Providing consistent support and positive reinforcement as children face their fears is essential. Celebrate their courage to compete, regardless of the outcome, and provide constructive feedback to help them learn and grow.

*Do I give my child positive reinforcement
and support when they face their fears?*

This approach reinforces the idea that fear is a part of the journey towards success, not a barrier to it. By recognizing and assessing fear, celebrating courage, and providing positive reinforcement in the face of fear, parents increase their child's comfortability with competition.

Through Competition ... Grace

Ironically, without exposure to competition and win or lose scenarios, it is very difficult to teach children the value of sportsmanship, respect, and humility. Seeing competition as a vehicle to cultivate respectful behavior towards opponents, coaches, and officials, regardless of the outcome, are products of participating in competitive settings. Specifically, competition can be a great way to teach core interpersonal values. Communicating these important outcomes to children can make them more willing to participate in competitive scenarios because the value of the competitive experience goes beyond winning and losing.

Do I emphasize the importance of sportsmanship and respect in competition?

Direct competition offers a powerful platform that presents as opportunity for children to cultivate important virtues like humility and grace. While competition is

93

rooted in winning vs. losing, play a role in teaching their child to handle victories with respect for their opponent and defeats with dignity.

How do I help my child win and lose with grace and humility?

Recognizing and learning from opponents is another benefit of competition. Teaching children to view their competitors as valuable contributors to their growth promotes respect and humility. Parents can encourage their children to reflect on what they can learn from their opponents' strengths and strategies, fostering an attitude of respect.

Do I encourage my child to respect and learn from their opponents?

By connecting direct competition as an opportunity to foster sportsmanship, humility, and learning from others, parents can help their children become well-rounded athletes who excel in sports and carry these important

values into all areas of life.

Checklist for Parents: Performance Mindset

Building Confidence

- ○ Do those in my child's sporting environment praise my child's effort and improvements rather than just their successes?

- ○ Are there opportunities for my child to experience both success and overcome challenges?

- ○ Is my child encouraged to take risks and step outside their comfort zone?

- ○ Are my child's small victories and personal achievements celebrated?

Developing Stress Tolerance

- Does the environment generate appropriate challenges that can enhance my child's stress management skills?
- Do coaches identify and develop effective stress management techniques, like positive self-talk?
- Does my child feel supported during high-pressure situations and that helps them cope with setbacks?
- Are failures and setbacks seen as learning opportunities?
- Is my child learning to identify their stress triggers and develop coping strategies?

Encouraging Competitiveness

- Is my child's participation developing their competitive edge?

- Is there a healthy attitude towards competition, emphasizing sportsmanship and respect for opponents?
- Does the environment help my child face their fears and overcome them?

By regularly reflecting on these questions, parents can ensure their child is experiencing an environment that fosters a Performance Mindset, helping them develop the self-confidence, stress tolerance, and competitiveness needed to succeed in sport and beyond.

The "I Am Capable" Mindset

An "I am Capable" Mindset is foundational to living a fulfilling life. It is a mindset that is grounded in one's ability to learn and grow, to set and achieve goals, and to take responsibility for their actions and decisions. An "I am Capable" outlook is rooted in self-efficacy and agency— where individuals are empowered to take charge of their lives and pursue their passions. When one sees themself as capable, they are more likely to set challenging goals, remain committed to achieving them, and recover from setbacks.

The "I Am Capable" Mindset emphasizes autonomy, goal setting, and accountability as key components for personal growth and success. It is important to foster the "I Am Capable" Mindset in childhood because it develops an internal locus of control in children, which can position them to direct their own lives and make meaningful choices that lead to a fulfilling future. Children who are challenged to develop an "I Am Capable" Mindset learn to take responsibility for their actions and decisions, are less likely to feel victimized by external circumstances, and more likely to see themselves as agents of change in their own lives. This leads to a sense of empowerment and self-determination that can be transformative.

Taking part in sport can be an effective way to foster the development of an "I Am Capable" Mindset in children. Sport provides an opportunity for children to develop autonomy and accountability by allowing them to make their own decisions and take ownership of their physical development. In team sports, children learn to work collaboratively towards a common goal and are held accountable for their role in achieving that goal. They also can take on leadership roles such as team captain or mentor, which helps to build their sense of responsibility to others. Finally, sport provides a structured environment for children to learn to set and achieve goals. Children can learn to prioritize their efforts and build meaningful strategies to achieve what is important to them.

Autonomy

Autonomy refers to the ability to make independent decisions and direct one's own actions. In child development, autonomy is foundational to self-esteem and self-efficacy. Children who develop a strong sense of autonomy tend to have a positive self-image and are more willing to sustain motivational efforts to achieve their goals. Autonomy also helps children develop a sense of control over their lives and allows them to make decisions based on their own incentives, leading to a greater sense of satisfaction and happiness.

In sports, fostering autonomy involves giving children opportunities to make choices about their training, chart their own course, and direct their performance. However, competitive sports can sometimes create an "autonomy trap" where children are constantly told what they need to do, how to perform, and what goals to pursue. This rigid structure, while aiming to optimize performance, can be counterproductive by stifling the child's ability to think independently and make self-directed decisions. Over time, this can lead to decreased motivation, and a lack of ownership over their athletic journey, and a reduced sense of personal satisfaction.

To avoid the autonomy trap, parents must strive to balance guidance with freedom. This means providing children with the support and resources they need while allowing them the freedom to make their own decisions. Encouraging young athletes to provide input, choose the skills they want to work on, and decide how to approach their training can foster a greater sense of ownership and intrinsic motivation. By promoting self-directed behaviors, children can develop the agency needed to navigate both their athletic and personal lives successfully. This approach not only enhances their athletic performance but also contributes to their overall growth and development.

Consider these strategies to promote autonomy through athletics:

Balance Guidance with Freedom

Balancing guidance with freedom is a perspective that promotes autonomy in young athletes. It manifests by parents taking a position that directs and provides the necessary support and resources while also allowing children the space to make their own decisions—and mistakes. Instead of dictating every aspect of their training routine, parents can encourage their children to choose the skills they want to work on and what strategies they want to utilize. For example, if a child is interested in improving a specific skill, parents can support this interest by providing the necessary resources, while allowing the child to decide when and how often to practice. This approach helps children develop a sense of ownership over their athletic journey and boosts their intrinsic motivation. When children feel they have control over their own development, they are more likely to be engaged and committed to their training.

Do I guide my child but also give them the freedom to make their own choices?

By allowing children to make decisions about their training and participation, parents can help them develop critical thinking and problem-solving skills. This process of trial-and-error builds self-efficacy and independence. When children make progress through their self-directed efforts, the sense of accomplishment is greater because the success is truly their own. This fosters a positive cycle of motivation, as children learn that their efforts and decisions directly impact their progress and success.

Remember freedom must be balanced with guidance; parents must identify and communicate when a child's strategies, effort, or execution is not aligned with their desired outcomes (but more in this when we get to accountability and goal setting—two critically important behaviors in establishing the "I Am Capable" Mindset.)

Resist Over-Correction

The desire to over-correct children can undermine their development of autonomy. While it may be tempting to step in and correct every mistake, this can limit a child's ability to learn from their experiences and make independent decisions. Over-correction sends the message that the child cannot be trusted to handle situations on their own, which can stifle their confidence and willingness to try.

Can I resist the urge to over-correct and allow my child to learn from their mistakes?

Instead of immediately providing solutions, parents can ask open-ended questions like: *What do you think worked well in that situation?* or *What could you try differently next time?* Encouraging your child to reflect on their performance or preparation and think about what they could do differently next time is an effective way to be involved without stifling autonomy. This approach encourages children to analyze their actions, identify areas for improvement, and develop strategies for future success. By allowing children to take ownership of their learning process, parents help them learn to handle challenges on their own.

Encourage Independent Development

Encouraging independent development is essential for fostering autonomy in children, both within and outside of sports. By promoting initiative, parents help their children develop the skills needed to take charge of their own growth.

Do I encourage my child to take initiative and develop on their own?

This not only builds self-efficacy but also empowers them to become proactive in their learning and personal development. In today's youth sport environment, children are rarely encouraged to engage in unstructured play. Too often, children are over-trained in highly structured environments, which can stifle their creativity and enjoyment. Allowing children to have free playtime, where they can experiment with new techniques and play without the pressure of performance can help them develop skills in a more natural and enjoyable way. This approach not only enhances their athletic abilities but also ensures that they remain passionate and motivated.

Do I encourage my child to practice on their own and incorporate play into their training?

Supporting independent development outside of sports can also enhance a child's performance within sports. Encouraging children to take the initiative in their daily lives, whether through pursuing hobbies or other activities helps build their sense of initiative. These experiences broaden their skill sets and reinforce the idea that they are active participants in their own development.

Goal Setting

It has been said that *if you don't know where you're going, any road will take you there*. It has also said that i*t's about the journey and not the destination*. Bridging these two worldviews is effective goal setting: identifying a vision and shaping a path to get there. Individuals who can set clear and meaningful goals are better equipped to create successful outcomes. They can break down large aspirations into manageable and measurable steps, prioritize their time, and recognize incremental gains to maintain their motivational persistence.

Introducing the practice of goal setting in childhood helps children learn to create a plan of action, prioritize tasks, and work diligently towards their objectives. As they practice setting and achieving goals, children develop a sense of ownership over their actions and begin to understand the relationship between effort and outcome—

that their progress is the result of their actions and hard work.

Sport provides an excellent platform for children to learn effective goal setting habits. The nature of sport involves a great deal of real-time feedback, allowing children to see immediate results from their efforts and adjustments. This constant feedback loop helps them understand what works and what doesn't, making it easier to set goals. Additionally, sport comes with many measurable variables, such as scores, times, and statistics, which provide clear benchmarks for progress and success. These concrete outcomes enable children to track their progress and stay motivated.

Consider these tips to encourage effective goal setting through youth sport:

Teach the Difference Between Aspirations and Goals

There is a difference between aspirations and goals. Aspirations are broad, long-term desires—guiding stars that shape a child's ambition and gives them a sense of purpose. Aspirations include becoming a professional athlete, winning a championship, making the "A" team, attending a certain university, or being team captain. They provide direction and keep the child inspired over the long-term. Yet without breaking these aspirations down into smaller, actionable steps, they can seem daunting and unattainable.

Goals, on the other hand, are the concrete steps that lead toward those aspirations. They are the tangible milestones that children can work on daily, making the path to their aspirations clearer and more achievable. For instance, if a child's aspiration is to become a professional soccer player, a concrete step might be to practice dribbling for 30 minutes each day. Parents can explain that while aspirations provide the overall vision and motivation, goals are the actionable plans that facilitate progress. This understanding ensures that children set targets that keep them motivated and focused on their progress.

Do I help my child distinguish between their long-term aspirations and the specific goals they need to achieve to get there?

Teaching this distinction is essential because it helps children stay grounded and focused. When children know how to break down their big dreams into smaller, manageable tasks, they are less likely to feel overwhelmed and more likely to stay committed to their efforts. This process not only boosts their confidence as they achieve each milestone but also fosters a sense of accomplishment that fuels their motivation to keep striving towards their aspirations. This also ensures that even if children do not reach their aspirations, their journey is still meaningful and full of accomplishment.

Ensure Goals Are Not "Just About You"

It is important to teach children that their goals should encompass more than just their personal achievements. They should also consider team goals, community goals, and other independent goals that contribute to a broader purpose. This perspective helps children understand that success is not solely about individual accomplishments but also about contributing to the well-being and success of others. By promoting a more inclusive approach to goal setting, you help a child develops a sense of responsibility and connection, fostering a more well-rounded character.

Do I encourage my child to set goals that
extend beyond their personal aspirations?

Team goals are a great way to help children understand the importance of collaboration and collective success. This could mean setting goals to improve team communication, support teammates in practice, or achieve a team milestone. When children see their efforts contributing to the group's success, they learn the value of teamwork and shared responsibility. This experience not only enhances their ability to work well with others but also teaches them to appreciate the contributions of their peers, fostering a sense of community and mutual respect.

In addition to team goals, encourage your child to set goals that benefit the community and involve independent pursuits that align with broader values. Community goals might include contributing a set time and effort organizing a local sports event, participating in charity runs, or volunteering for community service projects related to their sport. By diversifying their goals to include personal, team, and community outcomes, children learn to apply goal setting in all aspects of their life.

Accountability

To be accountable is to take responsibility for outcomes. In life, those who take responsibility for their actions and decisions are seen as reliable and dependable, making them highly sought after and valued in both personal and professional settings. As a form of self-discipline, accountability directs individuals to consider the impact they have on the world, and whether that impact is aligned with their motivation, goals, and expectations. Accountable people are more likely to follow through on commitments, learn from their mistakes, and continuously strive for improvement. This commitment to personal growth and duty to those around them builds trust with others and enables them to impact on the lives of others.

Challenging children to learn to take responsibility for their actions is foundational for healthy development—actions have consequences. As they grow, the tasks and duties that require them to be answerable for their actions grow in complexity and scope. These experiences teach children the importance of being reliable and following through on commitments. They also teach children the valuable role standards and expectations play in one's life. When children learn to adhere to standards and meet expectations, they begin to understand the broader implications of their actions and the trust others place in them.

Sport serves as an ideal vehicle to teach accountability. In a sports setting, athletes must take responsibility for their performance—individually and as part of a team. They learn to accept constructive criticism, own up to mistakes, and work towards improvement. This process instills a sense of accountability as athletes understand that their actions have direct consequences on the team's success. Additionally, sport provides a structured environment where children can practice accountability regularly, reinforcing these lessons through consistent application.

Use these tips to foster health accountability through youth sport:

Inconsistencies Between Expectations and Actions

Developing accountability in children involves pointing out inconsistencies between their expectations and actions. It is essential parents to make children aware of any gaps between what they set out to achieve and what they are actually doing to get there. For example, if a child wants to improve their performance in a sport but is not putting in the necessary practice time, gently pointing out this inconsistency can help them understand the importance of aligning their actions with the outcomes they expect.

Do I help my child see where their actions don't match their goals?

When parents point out inconsistencies between their children's expectations and actions, it should be about fostering awareness and foresight. As adults, parents naturally have the advantage of both experience and cognitive maturity. This allows them to see the longer-term consequences of actions—or inactions—that children might not yet fully grasp. Just as a parent is physically taller and can see farther down the road than their child, they are also mentally equipped to understand the connection between behaviors and outcomes. By gently guiding their child to recognize these inconsistencies, parents help them develop the foresight to understand how their current choices impact their future success. This method cultivates a child's ability to self-reflect and align their daily actions with their long-term goals, ultimately reinforcing the importance of accountability and personal responsibility.

Keep Accountability Healthy and Avoid Unnecessary Guilt

Healthy accountability promotes growth, not guilt.

Accountability should be about learning and improving,

not blaming for past mistakes or shortcomings. In times when it is appropriate to hold children accountable, emphasize that everyone makes mistakes and that these are opportunities for learning rather than reasons for self-blame.

Do I help my child distinguish between being accountable and feeling guilty?

Healthy accountability also fosters an orientation to seek out feedback, which is critically important to improving performance. When discussing performance, focus on constructive feedback rather than criticism. Highlight what your child did well and provide specific suggestions for improvement. Avoid language that might make them feel guilty or ashamed. Instead, frame your feedback in a way that encourages them to take positive steps towards their goals. For example, instead of saying, "*You didn't try hard enough,*" parents could say, "*I noticed your effort wasn't consistent throughout the whole game*".

It's also important to be mindful of the hindsight bias trap, where children might blame themselves for not foreseeing outcomes they couldn't have predicted. Help them understand that while accountability is about owning their actions, it's also about recognizing that some factors are beyond their control. This balanced perspective ensures that accountability remains a positive force for growth, helping children learn and develop resilience without feeling overwhelmed by guilt or unrealistic expectations.

Checklist for Parents:

"I Am Capable" Mindset

Encouraging Autonomy

- ○ Do I allow my child to make decisions about their sports and activities?
- ○ Does the sporting environment permit my child the space to make mistakes and learn from them?
- ○ Am I providing opportunities for my child to explore their interests and develop their skills independently?
- ○ Do I support my child's choices and celebrate their efforts to be self-reliant?

Fostering Goal setting habits

- ○ Does my child regularly set short-term and long-term goals in their sports activities?

- Do their teams create a plan of action to achieve their goals and prioritize tasks?
- Do I provide feedback and celebrate my child's progress towards their goals?
- Am I encouraging my child to adjust their goals based on their experiences and learn from their setbacks?
- Do my child's goals reflect personal, team, and community outcomes?

Teaching Accountability

- Is my child responsible for their commitments in sports and other activities?
- Does the sporting environment keep accountability healthy and not place undue blame or guilt for not meeting the mark?
- Do I teach my child to understand the consequences of their actions and behaviors?

- Am I encouraging my child to take ownership of their successes and mistakes?
- Does my child's sporting environment set clear expectations and provide consistent constructive feedback?
- Is my child developing self-awareness and self-reliance through their sports experiences?

By regularly reflecting on these questions, parents can ensure they are creating an environment that fosters the "I Am Capable" Mindset in their children, helping them develop autonomy, goal setting skills, and accountability. This mindset will empower children to feel capable in their abilities, leading to greater satisfaction and success in life.

The Fulfillment Mindset

The Fulfillment Mindset is a willingness to endure challenges while staying positive. It manifests as a deep sense of conviction and intensity in the face of adversity. Those who embody this mindset embrace challenges and setbacks as opportunities for growth and learning and can maintain an optimistic attitude even in challenging or uncertain situations. They understand that life is not always easy and approach challenges with a sense of purpose and an unwavering belief that they can overcome any obstacle. A Fulfillment Mindset contributes to long-term success because it builds motivational patience—the understanding that good things come to those who work hard while they wait.

Developing a Fulfillment Mindset in childhood sets the foundation for a resilient outlook. When children approach challenges with determination, discipline, optimism, and a strong sense of community, they are more likely to embrace challenges with an open mind and a positive attitude. By fostering this mindset early on, children learn to view adversity as a normal part of the learning process, helping them build the resilience needed to navigate life's ups and downs.

Sport provides an ideal environment for cultivating a Fulfillment Mindset in children. In a sports setting, children learn that achieving long-term success requires sustained effort and dedication and will certainly present setbacks and obstacles. The discipline, routine, and teamwork inherent in sports activities provide an environment where children can develop the essential characteristics of the Fulfillment Mindset and apply it in all areas of their life.

Determination

Determination is the unwavering persistence to pursue and achieve meaningful goals despite facing challenges and setbacks. It drives individuals to maintain focus and persevere through adversity, enabling them to reach their long-term objectives. Determination evokes an intensity when overcoming obstacles—an intrinsic motivation to keep pushing forward and bounce back from failures. With a Fulfillment Mindset, determination is not just about achieving success; it is about embracing the journey and finding satisfaction in the effort and progress made along the way.

The importance of cultivating determination in children cannot be overstated. It is a foundational trait for success in all areas of life, whether personal or professional. Determined individuals are more likely to set ambitious goals and work tirelessly towards them. They understand that success often requires sustained effort and are willing to invest the time and energy needed to achieve their aspirations. Those who are determined are more likely to seek solutions and adapt to changing circumstances rather than giving up in the face of adversity.

Sport provides an ideal environment for cultivating determination in children. In sport, children are regularly exposed to situations that test their resolve and perseverance. They learn that success requires consistent practice, hard work, and the ability to push through physical and mental barriers. Through training and competition, children experience both victories and defeats, teaching them valuable lessons about resilience and the importance of staying committed to their goals.

Use these strategies to reinforce determination through youth sport:

Frame a Setback for What It Is

Framing setbacks correctly helps children understand that challenges and failures are part of the growth process. When children experience setbacks, parents can frame these moments as opportunities for learning rather than definitive failures. By reframing setbacks, parents reinforce that obstacles are temporary and surmountable.

Do I help my child see setbacks as learning experiences rather than failures?

Open discussions are needed to reframe setbacks and uncover what can be learned from them. Ask questions like: *What did you learn from this experience? How can you use this setback to improve in the future?* This approach helps children be proactive in overcoming challenges. When children understand that setbacks are a natural part of their journey, they are more likely to stay motivated and determined to achieve their goals.

Never Underestimate the Power and Value of Effort

Effort is the driving force behind improvement and success. When children understand that hard work and dedication are at the core of achieving their goals, they begin to see their progress as something within their control. That is because focusing on effort aligns perfectly with a *"trust the process"* approach. Effort is something that requires no special talent—it's 100% within an individual's control. Whether a child is naturally gifted or not, they have the power to choose how much effort they put into their pursuits. This shifts the focus from fixed abilities to the amount of effort one is willing to commit. When children learn to value effort as the most important factor in their success, they acquire a powerful resilience mindset that believes in showing up consistently and putting in the work—results will follow.

Zoom Out to See the Bigger Picture

Helping children zoom out and see the bigger picture can sustain their motivational intensity and determination. Often, children can become overly focused on immediate setbacks and lose sight of their long-term progress and goals. By encouraging children to look at their overall progress, parents can help them maintain a balanced perspective.

*Do I help my child see the broader journey
and understand that setbacks are a
necessary part of development?*

Create opportunities for your child to reflect on their journey and recognize how far they have come. Ask questions like: *Can you think of a past setback that seemed overwhelming at the time but helped you grow? How did overcoming that challenge benefit you in the long run?* This reflection helps children see that setbacks are not just obstacles but essential steps in their development.

Keeping a journal or a record of their achievements and challenges can be a great way to recognize and appreciate the value of past setbacks. Reviewing this record periodically can help them appreciate their growth and stay motivated. Highlighting past successes and how they overcame previous challenges reinforces the idea that persistence and determination lead to progress. By zooming out to see the bigger picture, children can maintain their motivation and continue striving towards their long-term goals with renewed determination.

Discipline

Discipline is the behavioral expression of commitment and inner resolve. Discipline is motivational patience—the ability to remain steadfast while enduring the necessary efforts and time required to achieve long-term goals. It is about maintaining focus and consistency in one's efforts, even when faced with challenges or temptations to deviate from the path. This inner strength drives individuals to persevere, work diligently, and stay committed. Those who exude discipline understand that true achievement often requires sustained effort and self-sacrifice. Discipline is the backbone of a process-focused approach, emphasizing the journey and the quality of effort invested along the way, not just the outcomes.

Developing discipline in childhood is needed to set the foundation for lifelong success. Children who learn discipline early on are better equipped to manage their time and make responsible choices. Discipline teaches children to remain focused on what is important to them, even when faced with distractions, challenges, and competing priorities.

Sport is an ideal environment to cultivate discipline in children. It requires them to adhere to training schedules, maintain consistent effort, and make the necessary self-sacrifices to live up to their commitments and goals. To be successful in sport, athletes must practice discipline. Sport provides children the opportunity to learn motivational patience and commitment to see things through—no matter how long it takes.

Use these strategies to enhance discipline through youth sport:

The Way "We" Do Things

At the core of any disciplined individual lies deeply held values—beliefs that shape their worldview and guide their actions. Sports are a great way to introduce, instill, and reinforce important family values. Hard work, integrity, sportsmanship, leadership are all core values that can be shaped and reinforced through sport. Children can exercise a values-based lens to choose and prioritize their actions—even if that means making hard choices.

Do I help my child understand how values influence behavior?

Encourage discussions about how specific values can be demonstrated through sports. For instance, playing with sportsmanship and a positive attitude may reflect an important family value, which can be hard to maintain, especially in the face of poor performance or a significant setback. Ask questions like: *How did you show the value of sportsmanship during your practice or game today?* This helps children see the connection between their values and their actions, reinforcing the importance behaving in alignment with what is truly important to them.

A Commitment is a Commitment

Honoring commitments—especially the ones that are not enjoyable in the moment— is discipline in action. At times, if the environment isn't perfect or the results may not come quickly, parents might be tempted to allow their children to change course. However, it is crucial to teach children the importance of seeing commitments through to the end. Ensuring that commitments are honored, such as playing through seasons where performance, coaching, or teammates may not be ideal, instills a sense of commitment and resilience that can greatly benefit them in adulthood.

Do I ensure my child understands the importance of honoring their commitments, even when circumstances are less than ideal?

Every sports season is an opportunity to learn and grow.

Ask questions like: *How can you make the best of this*

difficult situation and still achieve your personal goals? This helps children focus on what they can control and make the most of their experiences, even when circumstances are challenging.

Highlight the long-term benefits of honoring commitments, such as building a reputation for reliability and developing a strong work ethic. Share examples of how staying committed, even in tough times, can lead to personal growth and future opportunities. By reinforcing the importance of honoring commitments, parents can help their children develop the discipline needed to succeed in all areas of life.

Optimism

In its rawest sense, optimism is a commitment to focus on positive outcomes. It involves maintaining a positive outlook and expecting favorable results. Optimistic individuals are more likely to approach setbacks as opportunities for growth and learning rather than insurmountable obstacles. Optimism fuels resilience that enables individuals to look forward and maintain progress toward their goals. Optimism also promotes problem-solving and proactive behavior, as individuals with a positive outlook are more inclined to take constructive actions to improve their situations. More generally, optimism is just good for you. Optimistic people tend to experience lower levels of stress and anxiety and are more likely to engage in healthy behaviors, such as regular exercise and maintaining a balanced diet. Optimism plays a key role in creating a fulfilling life.

Fostering optimism in children can play a vital role in their development. Children who learn to focus on positive outcomes and maintain a hopeful attitude are better equipped to handle life's challenges. Developing optimism in children involves modeling positive behavior, reinforcing their efforts, and helping them reframe negative experiences—which can be extremely challenging for parents! Parents can learn and teach children to recognize and challenge negative thoughts, replacing them with more realistic and positive perspectives. By fostering an environment that supports optimism, children can develop the mental habits needed to maintain a positive outlook throughout their lives.

Sport provides an ideal platform for cultivating optimism in children. Participation in sport offers numerous opportunities for children to practice maintaining a positive outlook, even in the face of challenges. To be successful in sport, children must reframe setbacks and failures as learning opportunities. Children can also practice optimism to make a positive impact on their teammates. By providing a structured environment for incremental growth and progress, sports help children develop the skills necessary to maintain a positive outlook and be successful.

Consider these tips to foster optimism through youth sport:

Challenge Patterns of Negative Thinking

Sports provide numerous opportunities to help children identify and counteract negative thoughts that can undermine their confidence and performance. Shifting the focus from what went wrong to what can be improved fosters a positive outlook and breeds optimism.

Do I help my child recognize when they are engaging in negative self-talk and guide them in reframing these thoughts?

Encourage your child to reflect on their thoughts after practices or games. For example, if they express disappointment over a mistake, guide them to see it as a learning opportunity. Ask questions like: *What did you learn from this experience? How can you use this experience to improve next time?* This helps children develop a constructive approach to setbacks, viewing them as steps toward growth. Additionally, look for common trends in how or why your child attributes their setbacks or failures. Identifying self-beliefs and patterns of thinking can reveal opportunities to shift their mindset towards a more positive outlook.

Parents can also play a valuable role by modeling positive thinking. Share your own experiences of overcoming challenges and the positive outcomes that resulted from staying optimistic. By consistently challenging negative thinking patterns and promoting a positive mindset, you can help your child build mental resilience.

Embrace the 'Glass Half Full' Perspective...Gulp!

Practicing a perspective that considers the "glass half full" helps children focus on positive aspects of their experiences and builds a foundation for optimism. Emphasizing the good aspects of their efforts and outcomes encourages children to maintain a hopeful attitude. One of the most popular movies with professional athletes (that has absolutely nothing to do with sports) is Dumb and Dumber. During a scene Jim Carey's character, Lloyd, asks his love interest Mary what are the odds of them getting together, to which she replies: *"about one in a million."* Lloyd's response: *"So you're saying there's a chance!"* Talk about unbridled optimism! The line resonates with professional athletes because Lloyd's optimism reflects the optimistic view they've had to adopt in many cases—they just needed a chance!

Do I help my child see the positive side of situations, even when things don't go as planned?

After a game or practice, highlight what went well. Celebrate small victories, like improved skills or teamwork, regardless of the final score. Ask questions like: *What were the highlights of today's practice? What did you enjoy the most about the game?* And: *what are you excited about for next time?* This helps children focus on positive experiences and reinforces their commitment to staying optimistic.

Gratitude can be a powerful tool in shaping a positive outlook. Help your child appreciate the opportunities they have, such as being part of a team, learning new skills, and having fun. Practicing gratitude shifts focus from what's lacking to what's present and valuable, promoting a sustained optimistic outlook.

Connect Optimism to Leadership and Support

Optimism as a leadership strategy reflects that one's actions can contribute to the cultivation of a positive environment. Teaching children that their attitude can influence and uplift others helps them see the broader impact of their mindset.

Do I encourage my child to use their optimistic outlook to inspire and support their teammates?

Encourage your child to be a source of positivity and encouragement for their team. Highlight the importance of offering words of support and encouragement to teammates who might be struggling. Ask questions like: *How can you help a teammate who is feeling down? What positive feedback can you give others?* This helps children understand that their optimism can have a ripple effect, enhancing the team's overall morale.

Fraternity

Fraternity, or the sense of belonging and connectedness to others, is essential for achieving success in life. It involves developing strong social bonds, a sense of community, and the ability to work collaboratively. These connections are vital for mental health, emotional well-being, and personal growth. People who experience a strong sense of fraternity are more likely to have better self-esteem, self-efficacy, and resilience, which are critical components for navigating life's challenges and achieving long-term success.

Promoting fraternity in young children enhances their development. Children who are given opportunities to participate in teams or groups are more likely to develop important social and emotional skills such as empathy and cooperation, which are necessary for building healthy relationships and navigating social situations effectively.

Sport provides an ideal platform to cultivate fraternity among children. Through sport, children interact with others and develop relationships based on trust, cooperation, and mutual respect. Team sports require players to work together towards a common goal, fostering a sense of camaraderie and unity. Effective communication and conflict resolution skills are also a benefit of the sporting environment, which are central to healthy social and emotional development.

Furthermore, sports offer opportunities for children to build connections beyond their immediate peer group. Participating in leagues and competitions that involve teams from different schools or regions allows children to meet and interact with peers from diverse backgrounds, helping them develop a sense of community beyond their own social circle and builds perspective by experiencing the broader world around them.

Consider these tips to facilitate a sense of fraternity through youth sport:

There's no "I" in Team

Teamwork is a valuable social behavior children learn through sport. Children are encouraged to value the contributions of their teammates and understand that success in sports often comes from collective effort, even if that means not getting exactly what you want or need. Promoting the concept that the sum is greater than its parts help children understand the power of teamwork and collective effort. Individual talents are important, but it is team synergy that leads to success. Teaching children that their combined efforts with their teammates create a stronger, more capable team fosters a sense of unity and connection.

Do I encourage my child to recognize and appreciate the efforts of their teammates?

Team-building activities and exercises are great ways to promote unity and trust among teammates. Finding opportunities to connect with fellow athletes outside of sport only strengthens bonds and fosters greater appreciation for the unique individual each teammate represents.

By orienting children to value the unique contribution of each player, parents can discuss the importance of each player's role in achieving the team's goals. Ask questions like: *What do you think makes each teammate unique and why are they important to your team?* This reinforces the mindset that **T**ogether **E**veryone **A**chieves **M**ore.

Encourage Empathy

Despite the aggression commonly associated with team sports like football, hockey, and other contact sports, the fraternity of a team environment is an ideal place to develop empathy. Through team sports children learn to be aware of their teammates' feelings and to offer support when needed. Fostering empathy helps children build stronger relationships and creates a positive, inclusive team culture.

Support your child to reach out to teammates who may be struggling, offering words of encouragement and assistance. Discuss the importance of being there for one another, not just during victories but also during challenging times. Ask questions like: *How can you support a teammate who is having a tough day? What can you do to make your team feel more united?* This helps children understand the value of being a supportive teammate and strengthens the bonds within the team— and sharpens their capacity to be compassionate and sensitive.

All Great Teams Are Built of Great Leaders

Team environments create unique opportunities for children to exercise and develop leadership behaviors. Great teams thrive not just on individual talent but the leadership qualities each member brings. Emphasizing the importance of leadership helps children understand that everyone can contribute to the team's success in meaningful ways. Parents can encourage children to take leadership roles, formal or informal, within their team. Discuss the qualities of effective leaders, like self-sacrifice and the ability to inspire and motivate others, while also recognizing a child's unique leadership strengths. Ask questions like: *How can you lead by example on your team? What can you do to support and motivate your teammates? What do you think makes YOU a good leader?* This helps children see that leadership is about serving others and contributing to the team's collective success.

Do I encourage my child to step up and demonstrate leadership within their team?

Checklist for Parents:
Fulfillment Mindset

Cultivating Determination

o   Is the sporting environment helping my child develop resilience by viewing their challenges as opportunities for growth?

o   Is the sporting environment supportive in a way that my child feels safe to try again after failures?

o   Am I modeling determination and perseverance in my own actions and attitudes?

Developing Discipline

o   Is my child engaged in activities that require regular practice and consistency?

o   Does sport encourage my child in sticking to routines and managing their time effectively?

- Does the sporting environment teach my child the importance of patience and consistency in achieving long-term success?

- Does the sporting environment reinforce the value of hard work and dedication through positive reinforcement and constructive feedback?

Encouraging Optimism

- Does my child focus on the positive aspects of their experiences and achievements?

- Is my child challenged to reframe setbacks as learning opportunities?

- Does their sporting experience foster a positive and hopeful outlook by celebrating small victories and progress?

- Do I model optimism and a can-do attitude in my daily interactions and challenges?

- o Is the climate of my child's sporting experience one that promotes teamwork and a sense of belonging?

- o Is my child developing healthy relationships with peers and mentors within their sporting experience?

- o Does my child's sporting experience create an opportunity for them to contribute to a larger community and feel connected to others?

- o Are empathy, communication, and mutual respect pillars of the learning environment?

By regularly reflecting on these questions, parents can ensure they are creating an environment that fosters a Fulfillment Mindset in their children. This mindset will help children develop the determination, discipline, optimism, and sense of fraternity needed for a resilient and meaningful life.

Embracing the True Essence of Youth Sports

Being a parent in today's youth sport landscape is undeniably challenging. The pressures and expectations can often feel overwhelming, and knowing what is best for a child is hard to discern. The "developmental dilemma" is a challenge that many sports parents face: balancing the desire to see their child succeed and achieve in sport with fostering a healthy and diverse childhood experience. Parents are faced with the hard choices: all-in early sport specialization, time and monetary investment, and chase 'the dream', or resist and live with the regret of not providing their child with the opportunity to be a successful athlete.

This dilemma is sustained by several misguided beliefs and practices. Many parents believe focusing on a sport from a young age is the key to future success. Many believe in the notion that more training and competition at a younger age is a prerequisite future success, or that if a child isn't showing early signs of greatness, they never will. These beliefs often lead parents to push their children too hard, invest excessive time and resources, and prioritize short term achievements over long-term development and well-being.

The reality is that early specialization is not a great predictor of long-term success nor a prerequisite to play at the highest levels of sport. In fact, those who do go on to achieve the highest levels of athletic success tend to have more diverse sporting and life experiences in childhood. Who would have thought that?

Knowledge is power. Knowing that a child's innate characteristics, talents, and abilities, guided by their unique developmental journey, will determine their athletic success can allow parents to take a breath.

Adopting a *"if your child is meant to, they will make it"*

mindset is an embodiment of the belief that a child's

potential will naturally unfold through their own efforts

and opportunities, rather than through forced

specialization and pressure.

By accepting this reality, parents can alleviate the

immense pressure and stress associated with trying to

control every aspect of their child's sports journey. This

mindset allows parents to focus on providing a supportive

environment where their child can explore, grow, and

enjoy the process of participating in sports.

To ensure that sport serves its intended purpose in a

child's life, the *Athlete Mindset* orients parents to what

really matters in their child's sports development: the

cultivation of skills and behaviors that will serve them on

their lifelong journey. These include the Performance

Mindset, which reflects an orientation to be self-confident,

stress tolerant, and competitive. This mindset develops

children to thrive under pressure, seeing challenges as opportunities to showcase skills and achieve goals. The "I Am Capable" Mindset, which emphasizes an orientation to be self-sufficient, autonomous and goal driven. This mindset ignites a capacity for children to self-regulate and take agency over their own life. Finally, the Fulfillment Mindset, which encompasses an orientation to be determined, disciplined, optimistic, and team focused. This mindset produces a heartiness of character in children that understands the pursuit of meaningful goals in life requires one to endure challenges with a positive outlook.

The bottom line: If a child's sports experiences are delivering returns on these mindsets, then sport is truly serving its purpose in their life. Whether a child is in a competitive specialized program at the elite level or playing at a recreational level, the best player on the team or the last pick, the coaches favorite or the kid that is currently getting overlooked for playing time—sport's true service to children and parents is through shaping these important mindsets and behaviors.

Knowing this, parents can relax and experience the joy youth sport can bring. Sport offers countless opportunities for children to growth, learn, and make lifelong memories—if parents can just let it.

An Open Letter to Parents

A great sport parent ensures that sport is serving the development of their child—not the other way around. They are focused on and steadfast in the pursuit of a positive and enriching experience that benefits their child and family both on and off the field. Their goal is not to raise the next superstar athlete but to nurture a happy, healthy, and well-rounded person who carries the lessons and values learned through sport into every aspect of their life.

As you watch your child grow and flourish in sport, remember that the greatest victories aren't always measured by trophies or medals or scholarships. They're in the moments of imaginative play where your child is pretending to be their favorite superstar. They are in the random games of pick-up that were never planned but turned out to be perfect. They are in the breakthrough moments of elation you both feel when they finally nail that skill they've been working so hard on. They are in the smiles and the tears, and the hugs shared in celebration or defeat. Embrace the joy of seeing your child discover their strengths and passions, and take pride in the person they are becoming. Let your heart be full of gratitude for every lesson learned and every challenge overcome, knowing that these moments are shaping them into extraordinary individuals. Be still and focused through the heartbreak. Allow your child to experience and grow through the suffering of loss, defeat, setbacks, injustice, and failures. These experiences, while painful, are integral to their growth and resilience—do not rob them of that. Be brave, for these moments, too, contribute to the amazing people they will become.

Most importantly, remind them that they are unconditionally loved. That there is no achievement that will make you love them more and not a single defeat or failure that could possibly make you love them less. Never forget that a big part of why children play sports is to be closer to you—so let them—let sport deepen your love for each other.

Parents —you're enough, too. Thank you for the countless sacrifices you've made to give your children the opportunity to experience sport, in whatever capacity you have been able to do. Your support, whether it's driving to early morning practices, working overtime, forgoing date nights and vacations—or simply cheering from the sidelines and being there with a comforting hug after a tough game—it is your dedication and love that are the true foundations of their success and happiness in this life.

Dr. Jay Harrison

August 2024